Storytelling:
A Guide
For Teachers

STORYTELLING:
A Guide
For Teachers

by Catharine Farrell

SCHOLASTIC
PROFESSIONAL BOOKS

New York □ Toronto □ London □ Auckland □ Sydney

Cover design by Vincent Ceci
Back cover photograph by Rick Gerharter
Back cover photograph hand-colored by Leslie Nicole
Illustrations by Leland Wong

ISBN   0-590-49139-3

Other editions:
Word Weaving: A Guide to Storytelling
© 1983 Zellerbach Family Fund
© 1987 Word Weaving, Inc.

12 11 10 9 8 7 6 5 4 3 2   1 2 3 4 5/9

Printed in the U.S.A.

Table of Contents

Acknowledgments 7

Preface.. 9

Me? A Storyteller? 15

Seven Steps: The Basic Technique 19

Telling It Your Way 28

Setting the Stage 32

Telling Your Own Story 37

The Formal Setting 43

One Teacher's Story 50

Stories to Tell 55

1. The Elves and the Shoemaker 56

2. The Three Bears (Traditional) 63

3. The Three Bears Jingle 70

4. Three Jovial Huntsmen 74

5. Ma Lien and the Magic Brush 77

6. Anansi the Spider, or How the Spider
   Got a Small Waist 83

7. Josefina 86

8. Daphne and Apollo 89

To the listener in each of us

Acknowledgments

Word Weaving, Inc., is a nonprofit educational corporation, established in 1987, whose purpose is "to assist educators everywhere by promoting and teaching the art of storytelling." I am indebted to each member of the Word Weaving Board of Directors—Evelyn Forrester, Joyce Gordon, Penny Hirschman, and Billie Jean Telles—whose dedication has formed our company and who have made the first editions of this publication a success.

I am particularly grateful to the Zellerbach Family Fund, San Francisco, William J. Zellerbach, President, and to all of the members of the Zellerbach Board of Trustees for their advice, guidance, and generous support over the years and for initially publishing and distributing this book.

I greatly appreciate the constant support of Gerald E. Marino, storyteller and business consultant. It is his belief in the value of storytelling and his legendary persistence that have brought this new edition into being.

I give special thanks to the young students in our back cover photograph, from Bret Harte Elementary School, San Francisco: (*left to right*) Jackie Wells, Christopher Lowe, Laura Virgin, and Nicole Wilburn.

Finally, my thanks to the Word Weaving trainers and educators for using the first editions of this storytelling guide in their workshops and for sharing their joy in telling stories with others.

Storytelling: A Teaching Tradition

ONCE UPON A TIME, NOT VERY long ago, there was a teacher who told stories to her class. She told tales of the small animals, and of the thundering herds in the sky, and of the fishermen three who sailed the skies with nets of silver and gold. Her voice filled the room with the cackle of witches and the whisper of ghostly sighs. She told of Lazy Jack and Clever Gretel and the well at the end of the world. She knew the stories of the make-believe places where dragons live. And she knew the true stories, too, about what happened in history or during a great adventure to the top of a mountain. And whenever she lit the story candle, she would light our eyes with wonder by telling a new tale or an old one we'd heard twenty times before. This is a story that will never end, for my memory of the teacher who told stories lives on, happily.

You, too, can become this unforgettable teacher! Educators certainly have the ability to become effective storytellers.

You only need to realize that there is no right or wrong way to tell a story: there is only your way. Your sincerity and authenticity are what engage students and are by far the most important aspects of classroom storytelling. It is your unique way of telling each story that will make it unforgettable.

The many advantages that storytelling has for our young students include reading motivation and active listening comprehension, a modeling of oral language, bonding, providing a safe environment for oral and written language sharing. Storytelling from the worldwide oral tradition celebrates our cultural diversity. Storytelling is cost-effective. It costs nothing at all—and it is priceless.

And as you prepare to tell stories to your class (your way), you can take comfort in knowing that you have a great deal of company. Down through the ages, storytelling was the traditional way of teaching. It is the most basic of the basics and reaches students at the beginning of their learning. Yet it has the simple power to appeal to students of all ages and abilities. This is seen most dramatically with students who appear not to be able to learn at all.

Storytelling can become the way to connect with disconnected students. You may ask why. How does storytelling break through to a natural way of learning when other teaching methods often miss? Part of the answer lies within the oral tradition itself.

Since time began, stories served to explain the world around us and presented truths in a way that was most like actual experience—that is, the consequences of action were experienced in the outcome of a story rather than in a didactic presentation. The symbols and metaphor of stories were the only curriculum for centuries.

With that in mind, we might say that storytellers were historically the first teachers. In a particular, long-ago tribe or village, the storytellers knew the explanations for the way things came to be and what would happen if things were not done correctly. These primitive "totem and taboo" stories soon developed into other story forms: myths, legends, fables and folk- and fairy tales. Later, epic cycles and hero tales became the cultural history of a people. Myths constituted their religion. Wise fables and folktales dramatized cultural ethics. Delightful *"pourquoi"* tales were the story science of all natural phenomena.

And so, the visual images of stories made up the common artistry of thought in our first way of knowing. Since these tales were not recorded, they were simply passed on in the oral tradition—over millennia. Similar stories were told and retold and are still told. Storytellers kept alive their culture's meanings for things. Stories spoke their truths and used their visual thinking. But since stories used images symbolically, all stories spoke a common human language. Their universal themes and motifs occurred throughout the world in many far-flung cultures. These stories became the thread that binds us all together, the past to today to tomorrow, the many cultures into one tapestry.

It is no real wonder that today's modern students can and do easily respond to storytelling, a holistic tradition of teaching that is as old as time. Our young children are also at the beginning of their learning. At-risk students and the child you find hard to reach often need the basic beginnings of thought and language told to them in stories. Simple and regular exposure to storytelling can provide the quantum leap into learning that these students require.

A teacher who teaches language-handicapped elementary-school children shares this recent storytelling experience:

> I told *The Mouse with the Musical Ear* with the intention of integrating music and literature. . . playing a few parts on my guitar, modeling for the students. . . . . A random student played the music with me afterwards using a

zither while I told the story a second time. . . . He played the music at appropriate times. . . . The entire class gave the boy a thunderous ovatio. . . . I received a note from him a few days later that said, "Dear Mrs. Obremski, thank you for choosing me to help you with the story. I don't usually get picked to do nothing in my class."

All students respond eagerly to the oral tradition! They love the closeness of the eye-to-eye contact, the heart-to-heart magic. Their bright eyes, enthralled by the storyteller's voice and vision, are motivation enough for you to learn the techniques of this simple craft. Yet beyond sheer enjoyment and immediate response, there are clear educational benefits that storytelling can bring—especially to our children today.

To skillfully use the integrated language-arts approach, the "whole language" teaching methods, we must start with the spoken word. The continuum of listening, speaking, reading, and writing begins with the voice. In this busy world, all too often students do not hear stories or even conversations at home. With storytelling, we are able to give students a dynamic first exposure to multicultural and classic children's literature long before they can read these same stories in print.

And as youngsters actively listen to stories told directly to them, they are visualizing, internalizing, identifying, and comprehending literary language. The interpretive use of language in stories is couched in symbol and metaphor, abstractions that convey multiple meanings. Though each student is listening with many others in a common experience, each child has his or her own unique vision of the story characters and setting. Each child is finding his or her own personal interpretation of meaning. This absorbed, active listening uses higher levels of creative, abstract thought.

Surrounded by television, movies, videos, and compelling, glossy images of all sorts, many of our students have lost their skill for visual thought. Yet we know that visual thinking is essential for all the language arts—listening, speaking, reading, and writing. Visualizing is as much a foundation for literacy as hearing voice in words: *students must be able to see what the words say.* Storytelling mentally stimulates students as they naturally begin to imagine and make sense of the story while they listen.

You as the teacher become the wonderful speaking model for imaginative, oral language skill. Using your own personality to tell stories, telling it your way, creates the impetus among students to speak in a similar manner.

This experience from a second-grade teacher demonstrates a natural response to teacher storytelling:

> This year I had an incredibly shy child who would never speak over a whisper. . . . Although she enjoyed reading, she did not communicate a great deal. . . . One day, Julie came up to tell me about a favorite story she had read. . . . She did not give me a synopsis. . . she told the story! . . . And she asked to tell it to the class. . . . Afterward, several children who overheard her telling it to me wanted to hear it in full. . . . Julie and three friends had their own little storytelling group on the playground by the end of the year!

Stories are entertaining; they are fun, playful. Before they know it, children speak the same language. The children naturally want to join in to repeat parts of the story or to play the story in a creative drama. Their speaking ability is greatly enhanced, and unique self-expression is encouraged.

Stories from the oral tradition touch students from other lands, other languages, as these stories speak a universal language. English as a Second Language students can appreciate the aesthetics in the stories told to them. Stories speak to the whole child. Students' ability to identify with the story characters and action is enhanced with storytelling. The teacher-storyteller has already internalized the plot and gives the ESL student added clues to meaning with gestures, facial expressions, and emotional subtext. Using folklore and literary stories that have special meaning for the bilingual student creates even stronger interest and comprehension.

An elementary-school librarian working as a storytelling resource to an ESL program shares this:

> The response to *Crow Boy* (by Taro Yashima, Viking, 1955) was particularly rewarding. The students responded strongly to the emotions expressed in the story. They identified with the main character's loneliness, being the object of name-calling, and being called stupid. The students were able to use written as well as oral language to express their thoughts.

Language benefits to all students in a cycle of classroom storytelling include the ability to express oneself in writing with a sense of voice and a clear connection to the audience/reader. Students exposed to storytelling can more easily read with a "sense of story," a knowledge of story syntax, language, character types, and probable outcomes. With an array of multicultural folk literature readily available, our youth can read widely from the oral tradition and begin to tell their own stories.

I hope that this small book will give you the beginning skills to a step-by-step process that will continue a great tradition of teaching. In the end, you will discover your own style and the stories you especially love to tell: personal stories, family stories, folktales, historical events, biographies, or literary classics. Whatever your educational purpose, whatever story you tell, may you tell it your way!

C.F.

Me?
A
Storyteller?

E ARE ALL A STORY, A LIFE STORY. We may see people's stories more clearly after they've lived them to the end, when we know how everything turned out. But stories are just as exciting in the middle, when we don't know what's going to happen—when we are living each day, page by page. It would be good to be able to share our stories with one another along the way. If only for the sheer entertainment of it, we might amuse each other with our predicaments and nonsense set aside in short stories, vignettes, anecdotes. But sometimes it's hard to know how to begin. So we mostly keep to ourselves and talk about the news, the weather, loose ends.

It doesn't occur to us that what happened just the night before might be interesting to anyone else. Maybe last night you were out grocery shopping with your three children and the collie in your compact car, and you ran out of gas on the way home. You and your kids and the dog jumped out and had a race down the road to the gas station for a can of gas so you could be back on your way before the ice cream melted. You had so much fun running with them—after you thought you were so tired you could hardly move—that when you finally arrived home you ate more ice cream than you should have and went to bed early, tired and happy. Another page of your book lived out, untold.

Now, some people seem to tell stories about themselves better than others. They're animated, amusing, entertaining, and so believable. When you listen to them, you're drawn right into the experience. Others tell jokes with such gusto that you hoot with laughter at the punch line. And still others can tell the plot of a horror movie they've just seen and set you on the edge of your seat, your throat dry. What enables one person to tell stories and events better than another, personality aside, is mainly the use of a few techniques that require some initial concentration. After you learn the basic dynamic that builds credibility, it becomes second nature. This is the art of storytelling.

This guide will give you the techniques of good story-telling you can use in any setting: office, luncheon, your child's bedroom, long car trips, or the classroom.

Story material is as endless and varied as all the peoples in the world. Every person has a story; every culture has a story. Many have been written down from the oral traditions of folklore and legend, myth and saga. This story material weaves the universal fabric of all peoples' common experiences. The old tales have lasted through time. Each contains a truth spoken in story form or a satisfying story design that works well and fills listeners with delight. And they often are the best choices for beginning storytellers. They're easy to select from book collect-ions. They're also removed from you, and you might not be self-conscious sharing them.

Children are the best beginning audience. If you already work with them, add storytelling to your program for their enjoyment and benefit. But don't limit your storytelling to the classroom or recreation hall. Use it at a staff meeting or at the next holiday meal with the whole family. Use it as a constant companion, warm, interesting, and inviting. If you are practicing the true art of storytelling, people seldom tire of listening. They'll stop what they're doing and fix a fascinated gaze on your face until, of course, the story's over. Sharing yourself in stories might become a habit, and you'll never regret it.

Shaping and framing are the keys to telling your personal experiences as stories. Developing your own style is important, too, so you know how to tailor story structure and content to your delivery. If you have a slow and quiet style, you might work best with a few well-chosen details, and leave the rest to the listeners' imagination. If you are a bright, quick talker, you might use a lot of detail for an embellished and just-as-interesting tale.

The truth is that each of us is a storyteller already. We've all had many experiences; we all know the old stories intuitively, if not by heart. Most of us have felt no one would listen because we feel that what we've lived, or what we know, is neither interesting nor important. But just the opposite is true. What we can share with each other—a living experience through a story—is the most fascinating way we can communicate. Storytelling can become the thread that weaves through our lives and binds us all together.

Reflections

1. Think of someone who listened to you talk about the events of your life.

2. Think of someone who told you about the events of his or her life.

3. Think of a teacher—not necessarily a school-teacher—who told stories.

4. Recall a special story from your childhood as well as you can. Think of how it begins, how it unfolds, how it ends.

5. Tell that story to a friend, to a child, or aloud to yourself, or record it and play it back.

6. Think of a story you know or one you've read that you strongly identify with. Find it and reread it carefully.

Seven Steps: The Basic Technique

LL GUIDEBOOKS PROMISE TO lead you from here to there. I want to take you along some well-trodden steps, the well-traveled corridor of gypsies and minstrels, troubadours and shamans, and sometimes politicians and con men. After all, many practice the art of illusion, though you and I know that stories truly shared are told from the heart.

I see seven steps to storytelling. Not every practiced storyteller does; some may see eight or three or five or none. But when I prepare a story, I find myself taking these seven steps. I've thought about leaving out one or another, but I always come back to this same set of steps, the arrangement that works ideally for me. It's not a long, winding staircase, only seven straightforward stairs—the kind that might take you up the front porch any day of the week.

Steps to Storytelling

1. Select a story you want to tell.
2. Learn the structure and block the story.
3. Visualize the settings and characters.
4. See the action taking place as if you're watching a silent movie.
5. Tell the story aloud, using your voice to project the images you've visualized.
6. Learn the story by heart, not word for word.
7. Practice telling the story until it comes naturally.

Each of these steps is equally important. Perhaps they appear laborious, but after you've told your first few stories, you'll find yourself skipping up the staircase, hardly looking. You might leap over all seven in a single moment of perception or recognition. However, let's start at the beginning, as Dorothy did on the yellow brick road to Oz.

Find a Story You Enjoy

There are countless collections of folktales, usually found in the children's section in a public or school library under the heading FOLK AND FAIRY TALES. Such books are excellent sources for delightful tales and are easy to learn to tell, because they are gathered from oral traditional literature.

Modern tales, written by a single author, tend to have plot sequences that are difficult to remember. The modern stories might be "decorated" for effect and have a superficial or "trendy" quality. They also are likely to be copyrighted, so storytellers must be careful to give credit to the author and respect the piece's style by learning it word for word. Remaining true to the text can be both difficult and restrictive. The old stories, on the other hand, have been smoothed by retellings until only the essentials remain. Though you often sense how these timeless stories are going to turn out, you want to hear them through to the end all the same.

As you search among the numerous sturdy folktales, find one that speaks to you personally, that you consider especially charming or unbelievably scary or wondrously exotic—a superlative tale to your taste. Your first story is going to be handled a lot, so if you thoroughly enjoy the story material, you'll like the learning process much more.

Learn and Block the Story

Read the story four or five times. Then draw its structure any way you wish—with a storyboard to show the scenes of the story; an outline to list its parts; three-by-five-inch cards, each with a separate section of the tale; a diagram; or a story map with arrows. Whatever form you use, you are now determining the story's structure—its shape.

Here are some examples of breaking a story into its constituent parts:

• "The Three Bears": two groups of three parallel events with a grouping of three objects in each.

1a. Goldilocks tastes all three porridge bowls
2a. Goldilocks sits in all three chairs
3a. Goldilocks lies down in all three beds

1b. Each of the three bears tastes a porridge bowl
2b. Each sits in a chair
3b. Each goes to a bed

• *Millions of Cats,* by Wanda Gag: a straightforward narrative of events from here to there and back again, held together by a refrain.

Cats here, cats there,
Cats and kittens everywhere,
Hundreds of cats, thousands of cats,
Millions and billions and trillions of cats.

• "Baba Yaga and the Little Girl with a Kind Heart":

1. Statement of the problem
2. Protagonist forced to confront problem
3. Protagonist receives tools for future use
4. Protagonist uses tools that match the difficulties exactly and therefore can overcome the difficulties
5. Solution of original problem

Put the structural work aside for the moment and reread the story, this time noticing and perhaps jotting down the scenes or locations in your story. If your story is "Hansel and Gretel," for example, you might select three basic settings: the father's cottage, the woods, and the witch's gingerbread house.

Visualize the Settings and Characters
When you've identified the story's settings, close your eyes and imagine each location as if it were a movie set. Forget the plot and the people for a moment. Simply look around the story. Notice small details. See color and light. You are invisible on the set. All your senses function except your hearing. For now, the imaginary world of your story is silent.

This exercise calls upon your powers of concentration and may produce sketchy results at first. But stay with it. If you can see only a few specific details, try to sustain them as long as you can. Suppose you can see the outside of the witch's gingerbread house with its frosted-sugar windows and pink, blue, and yellow icing. But when you open the door, everything goes dim. That's all right. Try to see one thing—the oven door, or the bed where Gretel sleeps—and leave it at that. With practice, you'll be able to open the door of the gingerbread house, walk in, pick up the herb jars on the mantel, sniff the brew in the pot, taste the jam on the kitchen shelf, notice the dust balls under the beds, feel the roughness of the bristles on the witch's broom.

Not yet allowing yourself to hear anything does hold your creativity in check. This is an artificial device, one I learned years ago from my storytelling teacher, Mae Durham Roger. Ruth Sawyer presents similar visualizing techniques in *The Way of the Storyteller* (Viking, 1942, pp. 142–144), though they're not original to her, either. Marie Shedlock considered storytelling a "miniature" with the "inward eye" being the "stage" (*The Art of the Story-Teller*, Appleton, 1915). For now, let's say that thinking of the story scenes as a silent movie set is a modern metaphor. The reason for silence will become apparent in the fifth step.

Now that you have a good mental picture of the setting, add the characters, going about their daily business. You see their mouths move as they talk, see them make facial expressions and hand gestures, but you can't hear their words. Notice their clothes, the colors, the expression in their eyes. With this third step, you have built and populated the world of the story with your own imagination.

See the Action

Now run the silent movie of the full story. Begin with the first incident of the tale and let the story action roll. If you can't visualize the story from beginning to end, keep trying: go back to your story-structure notes and start again. As you watch the story scenes move in exact sequence, get a feeling for which are fast-paced and which move slowly. Let the story build to its final and climactic scene, then let it wind down to the end. Switch off your mental movie projector.

Tell the Story Aloud

Using your voice is the most exciting and magical part of all. The reason you've been a silent witness to the story settings, characters, and action is to keep your creative focus on the visual elements. Your voice will now provide all the sound the story will ever have. It's the story's sound track: you will provide the descriptions, the narrative, the dialogue, the sound effects, and the music (or emotional tone). Now switch on the movie of your story again, saying your words aloud. Use your voice to project the images you are visualizing. Listen to your voice as you speak the dialogue, describe the settings, tell the action—all in your own words.

In good stories, the music of the words has rhythm and magic. Let some story phrases roll off your tongue. As you do, relish the sounds of the words and the way they resound in you. Try these:

> Once there was and there
> was not a king of Spain
> who loved to laugh.

> Cock-a-doodle-do! Turkish
> Sultan, give me back my
> diamond button.

> Benjamin, my husband,
> why are you standing
> there in the street with
> your mouth open?

Now tell your story over a few times, refining the expression of your voice to suit the words and reflect the story's images. Refer to your story notes as a cue.

A common alternative to seeing the story with the eye of

your imagination in order to learn it is to simply read the story aloud over and over, or tape the story and listen to the recording until you know the words well. That way you allow the words themselves to weave a spell. Merely sounding out the words of a story will call up in the listeners' minds their own images and strike the chords of their own feelings. Another way to internalize a story line is to type it out, slowly and carefully, seeing it turn again into print as if you were writing it yourself.

Learn the Story by Heart, Not Word for Word

Put your notes aside. Speak the story directly from your mental moving pictures. You already know the visualized events in sequence, so the story is memorized. You now know it by heart.

When you know something "by heart," you have internalized it. Take this approach to your storytelling and identify with the story itself. Deepen your connection with the motives of the story's characters and isolate the truth of your story, relating it to a truth within yourself. Turn on a tape recorder, close your eyes, and tell the story to yourself. Play it back just before you go to sleep or when you can relax completely and think about what the symbolism of the story might mean.

Your understanding of the layers of meaning in a story will greatly add to your telling of it.

Practice the Story Until It Comes Naturally

Tell the story to a tape recorder again while it's fresh in your mind. If you need to refresh your memory, play the story back to yourself. Join in with your own voice or simply listen to the tape and use what you hear—your own telling—to help clarify the visual story elements in your imagination.

The story is now ready to share. Practice telling the story to a live audience, if possible. Recruit your family, friends, or pets, tell it in front of a mirror or video camera, or record it on an audiotape when you perform in front of a live group. For further refinement, tell it while you're jogging, driving, or showering. A story is never perfectly performed, because it is always changing. Spontaneity modifies and adapts the telling to each new situation.

This step is the last of the seven, but the beginning of a never-ending storytelling process.

Finally, try out your story for the occasion you had in mind when you first chose it.

Reflections

1. Draw or write the structure of "The Three Bears."

2. In the structure of the story, highlight the climax, its culminating action, with a star.

3. Visualize the story of "The Three Bears." What are the dominant colors in that story? Why?

4. Describe the Three Bears' bowls in detail.

5. Describe Goldilocks in detail.

6. Speak the dialogue of the Three Bears when they return from their walk in the woods.

7. Tell the entire story of "The Three Bears" by heart (see page 63 for text).

Telling
It
Your
Way

OU MAY ALREADY HAVE TRIED
out or at least thought through the seven basic Word Weaving
techniques for learning to tell a story. What you'll discover from
here on, in your practice as a storyteller, will be your own.
Storytelling is a personal craft. The Word Weaving approach is
the one I use and teach, for it suits me. I enjoy preparing a
story if I can jump into the story world with my inner eye,
seeing each detail with a practiced clarity. However, this method
of visualizing may not suit you. That doesn't mean you cannot
become an effective storyteller. It simply means you will do it
your way.

There are many ways to render a story, from stylized
gestures (as in the Polynesian *hula*) to dance (the *Swan Lake*
ballet) to drum chant (American Indian) to simply using the
power of the word. Whatever you find yourself spontaneously
turning to is your way. You'll take in all the ways to learn and
tell stories, and they'll combine and reinforce each other until
you arrive at your own blend. Whatever method you've used to

learn your story, at the moment you tell it your personality becomes the most prominent interpretive ingredient.

Storytelling is a one-man show. Like the Dixieland jazz artist who himself plays the drum, mouth harp, and trombone, to name one of the possible combinations, the storyteller takes all the parts in the story. Every character speaks through the teller's voice; every animal squawks or roars; every sun rises and sets in the telling of a tale. Tone of voice, facial expressions, hand gestures, and body language express the story's emotions. All these are reflections of your personality as well, your unique style. The same story learned and told by five people often will be told in five different ways. As a storyteller, you'll discover your own style and soon become comfortable and secure using it.

Have you ever heard a duck quack? The duck is making a definitive statement—easily, clearly and with resounding conviction. Ducks have an air of supreme self-confidence and don't seem to care at all that they often repeat themselves. That same simple, clear delivery is the best way to start telling stories.

It's often frightening at first, so if you can think of yourself standing your ground on two (webbed) feet and saying it all the way through, it might help. You may make mistakes, get tongue-tied, even sputter and stop, but keep going to the end. This ugly-duckling phase, during which you may lack self-appreciation and self-image, eventually gives way to an elegant fowl of your own feather: you, a storyteller in your own right.

Begin by paying attention to your inclinations: Do you want to stand and have plenty of room for dramatic gestures? Do you want to sit in a big easy chair and invite people into an easy, intimate circle? Would you really rather be sitting on the floor? Will you move your hands to make a point? Should you take a moment in the story to pause and smile broadly, mischievously? Experiment with your own style, all the while concentrating on the story content. Expressions of your personality and the story should occur spontaneously and naturally.

You may find you like to stand quietly and tell the story straightforwardly, letting the story take center stage, your personality remaining a neutral backdrop. Or as you practice telling stories, you may feel a dramatic urge take hold and your arm suddenly stretch to the sky as one of your story characters prays to the sun god. Let these moments move you, take you into the dimensions of the story. You might discover something about yourself you hadn't known before or a part of you long forgotten. Let the story pull on you to find its expression, then follow your instincts.

Sometimes after a day of storytelling with different groups of schoolchildren I suddenly think, *I feel strange! Off and on through the day I've been a monkey, a crocodile, a ghost, a little red hen, a mouse, a cat, the man in the moon. I stirred soup and swam rivers and scampered on the highest branches of the swamp trees.* I'm not sure whether the characters have become me or I them, but we all enjoyed the respite together. A close-knit relationship between teller and story is a sure sign your personality is playing its part in bringing the story to life.

Reflections

1. What are your two favorite colors? Why?

2. Your favorite outfit? Why?

3. If you could be anywhere in the world right now, where would you be?

4. List the five words that most accurately describe you.

5. What animals are you partial to? Which ones frighten you?

6. Recall a time when you were very happy. What were you like then? Describe yourself as a happy person in that story.

7. Enter a dark room such as a closet, close your eyes, and listen to the sound of your voice. How does it make you feel? Accept your voice for what it is, and use it effectively.

Setting The Stage

STORIES NEED A STAGE, A CERTAIN framework in which they can be set aside, that marks their beginning and ending. The simple truth is that stories are made up of spoken words, ordinary speech, the same commodity we use when we order a new part for the washing machine. To signal that we now are going to "tell" and not "talk" takes some staging ability. Often that means looking for the right opening in a conversation, but sometimes "setting the stage" is more elaborate.

Children, especially, love to have a special event, even a story hour, ritualized in some way. We know this from their delicious anticipation for birthdays or for holiday treats.

Imagine the face of a child at his sixth-birthday party. Friends wearing birthday hats are standing around a table; the lights are off. Suddenly, the kitchen door opens and Mother walks out, carrying a birthday cake sparkling with six bright candles. Everyone begins to sing, eyes fixed on the burning candles and the face of the birthday child. "Happy Birthday to you. . ." What child doesn't love the magic of ritual, eyes closed tight to make the birthday wish, then extinguishing the candles with a mighty whoosh? What child doesn't carefully wrap the baby tooth that wiggled out of his or her mouth and hide it under the pillow? What child doesn't mark those special holidays on a personal calendar like beacons?

Setting the stage for a story for children could become as extravagant as you can imagine and still be thoroughly enjoyed. A classroom teacher, for example, might buy a story hat to put on whenever he or she is going to tell a story. In some cultures, the itinerant storyteller was known by a certain hat, sometimes adorned with charms: each charm was a story.

You could have a puppet introduce you and the story, or you might spread a magic carpet or rug where the children sit to hear the story. Perhaps you'll turn out the lights and light the story candle (a time-honored tradition) or ring a bell or chime to call attention to a special event: story hour. No children are going to think it's hokey—they'll get hooked on it. They'll offer suggestions, bring props or books from home, want to share their own stories, wear a costume from their wardrobe of old clothes. There's no limit to the appeal that stage setting has for children. When you have taken care to set a stage for yourself, you'll have their full attention. They'll hang on your every word.

The outdoors offers wonderful possibilities for story settings—perhaps under a spreading tree in the park, beside a granite cliff, or, best of all, around a campfire. Some settings, however, may look perfect but can present problems. The spreading tree in the park is wonderful until the power lawn mower shows up or the sprinkling system is turned on or the neighborhood fire station responds to a two-alarm fire. Long hikes are a good time for chatting, but storytelling needs a body at rest, alert, and ready to listen. Still, some of the most memorable stories for children are told outdoors. Closer to earth, sky, and animal, words seem to resonate. Here, the circle of listeners around a fire at night needs no further staging. At a word the story leaps, full-blown, out of the coals.

Holiday gatherings are times of ritual for children and adults. They are rich opportunities for storytelling, sharing common memories, reliving family histories. Perhaps after the big dinner has been eaten and all the dishes cleared, while the family is lounging in the living room, you might say, "Grandpa, do you remember the time way back when you first came to this country? And you didn't have a job or a roof over your head? Tell us about it. What happened? What did you do?"

Stories shared across generations are powerful messages. If you're a grandparent, your position in the family gives you the authority to tell the story of your life. Our cultural growth has accelerated so rapidly that a life incident 60 years past has an old-fashioned tinge to it, like a photograph from another era. The details of a grandparent's youth are truly historical now, so their stories have a kind of "weight of the ages" about them. Whatever story a grandparent or great-aunt or uncle tells is going to have an impact. If the older members don't know the prerogatives of their age, encourage them to perform this rite of passage: to tell the memorable stories of their lives to the younger members of the family. And as they tell, coach them. Ask for details, for their feelings at the time, for the lesson they learned from that experience.

Storytelling in an informal setting does need some direction so the group will know that Grandpa, for instance, is not just "talking" but "telling," and that something different from the usual after-dinner conversation is going on. The teller probably should try to catch the eye of everyone in the group and announce that he is about to tell a story. "Now, do you all really want to hear about the long ship ride that took me around the southern tip of South America and brought me to this country back in '06, penniless and out of work? Well, if you do, just listen." Old-time storytellers or just plain old-timers are famous for knowing how to "frame up" their stories to get you to listen.

Imagine this scenario: the old codger puffs on his well-worn pipe and leans back as far as he can in his rocker. As he takes his pipe out of his mouth there seems to be a twinkle in his keen old eyes. He leans forward and says, "Now that reminds me of a story. . . ." Even the cliché "When I was your age. . ." might be the simple opener for an astonishing tale. Imagine your great-aunt sipping a glass of sherry and saying, "Crisp, cool days like this always remind me of when I was a girl and the fall I got lost in the cornstalks and found my way to a small lake by the woods. . . . I'll never forget what I saw there. . . ."

It's true that the older you are, the more authority you automatically command as a storyteller. But don't wait for old age to creep into your bones before you begin telling your own stories. Telling them simply and unpretentiously in the context of your own daily life is enjoyable at any age.

Reflections

1. Think of a perfect opportunity to tell a story to a child you know well.

2. Think of a superb setting indoors or outdoors in which to tell a story to a group of children you know.

3. Think of a way to ask an older person, related or not, to tell a true-life story.

4. Think of a lavish storytelling ritual.

5. Think of a simple one.

6. Think of a way to make storytelling part of a family holiday or celebration.

7. Think of a way to make storytelling a part of classroom activity.

Telling
Your
Own
Story

HINK OF YOURSELF FOR A moment as a *bon vivant, a raconteur,* a connoisseur savoring your own life. When you think about it, no one is going to fully enjoy your life except you; and no one will know why they should unless you tell them. No one in this culture is likely to ask you to tell them the story of your childhood, or reveal the most embarrassing moment of your life, or explain why, to this date, you get sick on clam chowder. Most people don't think such information is interesting. You'll find, however, if you are discreet, that telling your stories can make you a fascinating, authentic personality.

I remember that all through my young adult life I was embarrassed and humiliated by my childhood. I didn't want anyone to know where or how I was brought up; it seemed impoverished, backward. Later, as I began to meet successful people, some rich people, I found if I scratched the surface of their lives, I often discovered a background of poverty and struggle. The hard fact came home to me: most people are not born with silver spoons in their mouths. Over the years my shame has turned into a recognition and acceptance of everything that shaped and influenced me. They are simply part of who I am and the story I make of it. Telling about my important people, places, and events is a way of celebrating and savoring my life.

Whatever has happened in your life, you've survived, so in a certain way, every story in your life has had a happy ending—you're here to tell about it. A compelling aspect of war stories—when people used to tell them regularly—was the relish of being the teller. A tragedy on the battlefront became an adventure in the telling. Your most miserable moments are worth telling because you've lived them. It can be like "singing the blues"—by the time you're singing them, you're on the way up. No one should think storytelling is only about the good times; it's about all the things worth remembering in your life.

Now, what if you have lost track of your story line? Where did it all start? Where is it going now? To get a sense of yourself and your own life story, take some time out to reflect. Find an island of time where you can be alone with your thoughts for an hour. Turn off distractions—the radio, the television. Just listen to yourself. Let your mind ramble comfortably for a while, then try to remember back as far as you can.

Recall your first memory, not what your parents have told you, but what you recollect. Fix that memory. Try to visualize it and sense as much as you can about it. Concentrate on the details of people, setting, dress, furniture, smells, temperature. Summon tactile sensations: were your socks itchy, your hands sweaty? Recall your emotions: what feelings did you have? What did you say? How did you feel about the other people who were there? Remember as much as you can, then relax, let go. Let the images fade and vanish. This is hard work, but an important beginning.

Replay your sense impressions of your "first memory"

again. As you do, think of the beginning of the incident. What was the beginning? How would you start if you were going to tell it as a story? You probably would want to introduce it with a few details of place, time, your age, and the others involved and their relationships. This gives your story a context, a setting, and characters. Continue to the incident, the action. What was so vivid about it that made it worth remembering? Describe the incident in detail. How did it end?

Now comes the most interesting part: the conclusion. What does the story say about you, or what did you learn from the incident, or what did you learn about yourself in telling the story? There can be many conclusions: draw one.

As you build a repertoire of true-life story material, make it a practice to set aside time to quietly reflect on the incidents of your life. The more accurately you remember information, the more vivid your storytelling will be. There's nothing like authentic detail: The listener can feel the truth of a chance detail all the way to the bone.

Use the following exercise to pinpoint *accurate* information:

1. Choose a year in your life, any year.

2. With the date in mind, gather whatever memory aids you have available: a photo album, old family correspondence, childhood toys, family history records, heirlooms from that time.

3. Close your eyes and recall images of that year. Let them flicker off and on at random, then look for important events of that year. Choose one incident.

4. Spend some time focusing on this incident. See it, feel it, use all your senses. Feel your emotions and physical sensations. Think your thoughts. Draw your conclusion.

5. Frame the sense impressions into the words of a story. Introduce the story, begin it, follow it through the action, end

it, and tell what it all means.

6. Jot down the story in your story journal. Use your own code or shorthand. Use sketches or other visual cues that will unlock your memory of this story.

7. Tell the story to a close friend. As you do, use your imagination to conjure up all the images, details, feelings, and sensations that were part of the original event. Tell it, don't talk it. For telling, the event must be well-lit with a freshness and immediacy, as if it were happening this moment. Remember the old opener "I can remember it as if it were yesterday." Use it.

Now that you've gathered all this story material, what will you do with it? First, you can realize that you are interesting. Your life is filled with color, feelings, drama, nuances, beauty, fear, dread, joy, misery, and pain, as well as with special objects, favorite hats, and worn-out teddy bears. And here you might have thought you were boring or didn't have any stories to tell. Next, you want to blend your stories naturally into everyday conversation. You don't want to bore everyone with your true-life stories. That's done by people who want everyone else to think they're interesting, but who don't think so themselves.

Suppose you're at lunch with a few friends, a time and place when most any topic can be discussed. Await a conversational opener for one of "your" stories: a key word, a parallel feeling, perhaps a chance remark. Train yourself to pounce on the opener. You might appear quizzical for a second and say, "Isn't that funny, I remember my father telling me something like that when I was a child. I had just come in the house covered with mud. . . ." The most important point to remember now, once you've launched into your story, is this: Turn on the lights, camera, action, feel it, see it, place the characters and action in midair between yourself and your listeners. Don't talk about it, tell it. Live through it again. Then enjoy your companions' reactions.

As you practice the subtle art of conversational story-telling, use it for every occasion, business and social. If you can use a story to prove a point, you'll be both entertaining and convincing. You might even begin to earn a reputation for being wise.

Reflections

1. Think of a way to teach a lesson on the seasons of the year by telling a story.

2. Think of a way to tell someone they just hurt your feelings by telling a story.

3. Think of a way to introduce a speech on fire hazards by telling a story.

4. Think of a way to ask a group of children to get along with one another by telling a story.

5. Think of the funniest story you have ever heard. Jot it down. Tell it at the first opportunity.

6. Think of the saddest thing that has ever happened to you. Find a safe way to tell that story.

7. Think of the most mysterious thing that has ever happened to you, one you still can't figure out. Tell that story at an appropriate time. See if you find an answer.

8. Tell a story about yourself using the third person.

The Formal Setting

O MATTER HOW AT EASE YOU become as a conversational storyteller or how quickly you win your colleagues' interest with a well-chosen anecdote, you'll still feel awkward the first time you tell a story formally. Everyone does. You may learn to enjoy your moments in the spotlight, but not before you overcome the stage fright. After all, a storyteller is a one-man band—everything depends on you. The story with all its people and events must come to life through your voice and inner responses. The art of storytelling itself puts you on the spot.

Imagine this scene: it is open-house night at school; parents are visiting their children's classrooms, talking with their teachers. The school bell rings to announce the scheduled assembly for the evening. Parents, children, teachers take their seats in the auditorium. The principal announces a special treat, a storytelling guest: you. You walk on stage, look at the many upturned faces, and clench your sweating hands. Except for a few creaky chairs, the auditorium is silent. What are you going to do? You feel unable to speak.

Let's leave you on the stage for a moment and discuss first what you are not going to do. Storytelling is not a dramatic recitation. Telling a story is at the same time easier and more difficult than a recitation. A dramatic recitation implies memorizing a piece verbatim and giving it "in character" (such as Hamlet's soliloquy), but storytelling demands that you re-create an entire living experience as a credible narrator, not as an actor. That means you have to establish a bond with the audience as someone both in the action as well as a commentator on the action. Therefore, you cannot lose yourself in the "theater" of the action, through extravagant gestures, props, or elaborate costumes, for example. Storytelling operates with the "power of delicate suggestion. . . . This is hampered by the presence of *actual things*" (Shedlock, pp. 31–32). Storytelling shouldn't be staged. Still, there is a simple solution. Let's return to you, standing, sweating, on the stage.

The best way out of the fright and the only way into storytelling technique is to make personal contact with the audience. You are not an "act" or someone who is "in character"; you can and must establish a direct, natural rapport with the listeners. Look directly into someone's eyes and smile. Then look around the group, making eye contact and smiling. Feel how it feels to be standing in front of the group. Breathe easy. All this has taken only seconds.

To maintain a natural relationship between yourself and the audience and to give them some time to become accustomed to you, introduce your story with a few anecdotes. You might tell why you chose the story, its special meaning for you, its meaning for that night, or something about its cultural origin. You might tell a very short "throwaway" story that echoes something in the main story, simply to continue building rapport with your group. As you've probably guessed by now, the audience is an important element in the creative process of storytelling. They soon will become eyewitnesses to your story. They need to warm up to it and to you so that when you do begin the story, your personality can fade away into the interpretive elements of the story itself. Pause.

Now it's time to begin. Give your story a title or identify it in some way, such as, "This is a tale of the Blackfoot people." Pause. Let your eyes sweep over the entire room. When you feel silence, anticipation, in the room, don't hesitate.

Tell the first sentence of your story in a clear voice; the first sentence frequently presents important clues to the rest of the story. Often folktales begin in the middle of the problem. Before you know it, the gazelle is talking to the beggar, or the cave on the side of the mountain is opening up for a band of forty thieves. The beginning of a folktale (one from an oral, not a written, tradition) is like the banner headline on a newspaper's front page. That opening information is crucial: now hear this!

Once you're through the first few passages and can start breathing again, remember to visualize. Click on your mental movie projector and begin to conjure up all the detailed images that make stories easy to remember and tell. Concentrate on setting, action, each character in turn, and the appropriate tone for each character's dialogue. But don't worry, this is not an act, and there is no exact way to do it—there is only your way. If you miss a part of the story, leave it out. Try to fit that information in naturally at another point, if it's necessary to the plot. A few mistakes are part of this tradition. As with blown glass or handwoven cloth, imperfections, personal touches, add to the value. Carry on.

When you come to the end of your tale, end it. Say nothing else. Pause. Wait for the applause; it will come. Again, greet the entire audience, smiling, using sweeping eye movements that include everyone. Bow. Leave the stage. The story has been told. There is no need to talk about the story after it is told—it has spoken for itself.

Imagine another storytelling scenario for yourself: A retirement dinner has been planned for one of the oldest and most respected members of your staff. You've been asked to put together some reminiscences about his early days on the job by interviewing other old-timers. You'll use what you gather to make an after-dinner presentation, taking the part of a pretend eyewitness to the old stories. The first of the seven basic storytelling techniques—selection—has been done for you.

Juicy gossip certainly will provide amusing material, but your doubts start to surface immediately. Will I remember it all? Will I make each incident come to life so others will relive the old memories? And will I appear a credible witness? Now use the other six steps to support you.

Be sure to group your stories so they build to some conclusion—either as examples of a certain character trait or as incidents leading up to a finale, or some other way that makes sense to you. Then spend time reading through the story material, seeing each event take place with the eye of your imagination. Rehearse your stories to anyone who will listen: your children, your dog, anyone.

Personal connection is the key that will make your stories work. Try for a conversational tone that invites the listeners into the recollected experiences, almost an over-the-fence intimacy. You'll be surprised at the effect of a simple, low-key account of true-life events once you've established a natural rapport with the group. Everyone will feel that you are talking directly to them.

As you speak, keep your inward concentration on the visual images of each incident, as if you were remembering something that just happened the other day. Pause from time to time. Digress. Forget what you were saying, then remember. Repeat yourself. Be leisurely. The stronger the bond you create with your audience, the safer you'll feel to be the most effective storyteller of all: natural, authentic.

If you are a teacher, your classroom can be just as intimidating as the banquet hall. No pictures, no movie or TV screens, no illustrations; a story might seem like a sure flop. Once, in one of my first library programs, I had chosen the English folktale "Cap O'Rushes," a 24-minute story that is a variation of the Cinderella tale.

As I watched the children take their seats, I thought, *They aren't interested in an old-fashioned folktale with kings and queens. They'll never listen to this.* . . . Somehow I found my courage. I waited until I had the full attention of the group, introduced my story, looked around at everyone in the room, and began, "Well, there was once a rich man, and he had three daughters, and he wanted to see how much they loved him. . . ." The class continued to listen as the story took hold and spun out into thin air. Then the story was over and they all had listened. I wish I had counted how many times after that they said, "Tell us 'Cap O'Rushes.' Tell us the story of 'Cap O'Rushes.' "

The warmth and intimacy of a small semicircle of children is hard to beat. But not every story time is as magical as my first telling of "Cap O'Rushes" was. Sometimes there are interruptions: a fire drill, a tardy student, a message from the office. Here are some tips that will keep the experience intact as you tell stories to children in any setting:

1. Find a quiet place for storytelling.

2. If possible, post a sign that keeps intruders out: STORY TIME—DON'T DISTURB. Or perhaps post a student or aide near the door.

3. Create a special ritual for story times—a hat, a bell, a gong, a candle, to mark both the beginning and the ending.

4. Once the story has started, don't interrupt it. Do not stop telling the story to discipline or explain a word or answer questions. If the children are noisy, speak more softly. The

tendency is to try to raise your voice over the group to hold its attention, but it will have just the opposite effect. Let them strain to hear you.

5. When the story is over, stop. Pause for spontaneous reaction from the group. Close the story hour.

Some of this framing, this formality, might seem artificial at first, but you soon will see, with experience, how important it is to create the optimum listening environment for a story. You already have given the story a great deal of concentration to be able to tell it—you don't want your efforts to be wasted on the desert air. Give the story an environment where it can thrive and be appreciated.

Stories, of course, provide rich material for language-arts activities. When you tell a group a story for the first time, a formal setting is best. Frame the story so it can tell itself. Let the listeners simply hear it. After a while, tell the story again, informally. Use it as a reading story for retelling and reading. Act it out. Write it down. But let the first telling sink in undisturbed for what it is:

> A story, a story,
> Let it come, let it go.
>
> If it be sweet,
> If it be not sweet,
> Take some elsewhere,
> And let some
> Come back to me.

Traditional African sayings from *A Story, A Story*, told by Gail Haley (Atheneum, 1970).

Reflections

1. Imagine the storytelling costume that best expresses your personality.

2. What costume, if any, would you wear to tell "The Three Bears"?

3. Think of a formal setting for storytelling at a scout meeting.

4. Imagine an adult audience for storytelling. How would you arrange the storytelling "theater"?

5. Think of a way to use a prop or two without detracting from the storytelling process.

6. Imagine a way to use puppets in your storytelling without drawing undue attention to the puppets.

7. Think of all your reasons for being afraid to tell a story, any story, in a formal setting. What is the worst thing that could happen? Name all your fears. Do you want to tell a story more than you fear to tell it? If so, your fears then become your companions.

One
Teacher's
Story

LONG AGO, WHEN I BEGAN
teaching, I had no idea of the power of storytelling. It was in
the mid-sixties; I was a brand-new and dewy-eyed high school
English teacher assigned to a difficult campus in San Francisco.

You can imagine my concern when no students arrived
the first week of school. It was the end of the long, hot summer
of 1966; part of our school community was on fire. The students
were afraid to come to school. The quiet, empty second-floor
classroom provided me with ample time to reflect. As I leaned
out the open window, listening to sirens across the freeway, time
seemed to hang suspended. What would it be like when the
students finally came to school?

Everyone still attended school in the mid-sixties, and our
shabby, green classrooms were filled with thirty to forty-five
students in each class. Though I felt well prepared to teach my
subject (with an undergraduate degree in world literature, a
minor in language arts, half the course work for a master's
degree in English literature, a year's worth of student teaching,

and a California secondary teaching credential), nothing prepared me for what I was soon to discover. Most of my seventh-, eighth-, and ninth-grade students could not read or write at their grade level.

How could I possibly teach the mandatory literature selections in the class syllabus, give composition assignments, or lead class discussions? I did not question why my students could barely read or write; I just knew I had to deal with this situation—and right away. I liked the students. Somehow we would "cover the material."

My immediate solution was, "Well, they can't read; I'll read for them." Though this had not been presented to me anywhere as a teaching method, I began to read aloud. Standing at the flimsy, plywood lectern (made by the woodshop class), I read aloud from the assigned grade-level texts: *Arabian Nights, Old Yeller, Great Expectations,* and Greek mythology. I became an inspired read-alouder. Gripping the lectern edges, I held sway over my classes with my dramatic interpretations.

I discovered that once the students knew the material, they had fascinating responses. We enjoyed many in-depth class discussions of our literature selections, which, as you may know, are what English teachers live for. I couldn't discern whether my students were reading or writing any better, but they could discuss the literature they had heard with a clear and lively understanding. It looked as if we would make it through the year after all.

But what was my first and obvious solution soon became boring and repetitive. I began to wonder if my voice would hold out, then to marvel when it did. I was reading aloud daily and for hours at a time. (Later I learned that the voice box is a muscle and that the more you use it, the stronger it gets.) I tried what is now known as Readers' Theater, but what I called then "taking parts of the story" or "let's make a play." With the students seated at their desks (always), those with some expressive reading ability took the parts of characters in the literary selection. This effort met with some success. However, my boredom with reading aloud continued.

One day in the spring of my first year of teaching, I prepared to read aloud a Greek myth to a ninth-grade class. These students were especially interested in the stories of Greek mythology and for that reason we had spent weeks studying them. But I couldn't stand to read another story aloud. Irked at the tired textbook prose, I stepped away from the lectern and the book. I stood in front of the class. The class looked at me with some apprehension. I began to tell them in my own words the tale next in the book, the story of Daphne and Apollo.

I will never forget the change in the room; suddenly there was nothing else in it except my words and the students' eyes, watching. They were looking at me with the greatest attention I had ever received, but at the same time I knew that they were not seeing me at all. They were seeing beyond me into the myth. In fact, both the students and I were watching the adventure of Daphne and Apollo as it took place. The shared experience of telling the story was far more immediate than reading it aloud from behind the lectern. The classroom itself was transformed; it seemed to become the far-off Greek forest of long ago, with tangled green foliage and splashing streams. For the length of the story, we were there! It was electrifying. And I was no longer bored. No, I was never to forget that day's experience.

I wanted to do more of that, whatever "that" was—for I did not even know the word *storytelling*. However, I knew if I did "that," the students would be remarkably quiet and attentive and I would be challenged creatively. I began to use "that" to teach my history and social-studies classes by relating the material from that day's chapter as if it were actually happening. I had no idea that I was storytelling.

It was while working towards a master's degree in library

science at the University of California, Berkeley, in the spring of 1970, in a class entitled Oral Interpretation of Children's Literature, that I discovered what "that" was. The oral tradition of storytelling was alive and well in the children's programs for public libraries. And I learned it. But I already knew its power.

When I returned to the San Francisco schools as a district librarian, I told stories as part of the elementary-school library programs. All the time, I knew how powerful storytelling was as a teaching method. It has long been my wish to share what I have learned about storytelling with classroom teachers and educators everywhere.

For more than ten years, the Word Weaving Storytelling Project, begun in 1979, has provided that wonderful opportunity. As I have trained hundreds, thousands of teachers in storytelling, I have seen my first stunning experience repeated many times over. Teachers who never thought that they could tell stories or who had no idea of their own style found they had a natural talent for storytelling.

So, I literally stumbled into storytelling without knowing the tradition even by name. And my students were rapt. I know that you can benefit from my first experience and tell stories in and out of school with great success.

But what next? You may wonder how to use the wonder of story time in your whole-language-arts curriculum. The following section adapts storytelling as a teaching method to the K–6 classroom with examples of stories and activities. Try a few or make up your own. The possibilities are endless, the source of stories seemingly infinite. As you begin this teaching tradition for yourself, it is your personal touch, your way, that will bring a story to life.

Stories to Tell:
Story Plans and Classroom Activities, K-6

The following selections of stories and classroom activities include the text of several stories and related lesson plans, K–6. There are hints for successful tellings in an introductory section to each story called Notes to the Teller. The classroom activities integrate the language arts with some extensions across the curriculum.

The stories themselves can be told at any grade. Most stories from the oral tradition are ageless and timeless; anyone can enjoy listening to them, appreciating them in some way. The activities in the story lesson plans, however, are graded for suggested levels. I hope that these stories and activities are merely examples that start your own creative process. Adapting storytelling to your own curriculum needs is another opportunity for spontaneous design in teaching.

The Elves And The Shoemaker

THERE WAS ONCE A SHOEMAKER who made shoes and made them well. Yet luck was against him, for although he worked very hard, he became poorer and poorer until he had nothing left but enough leather for one pair of shoes.

That evening he cut out the leather for the last pair of shoes and then, after laying the pieces in a neat row on his workbench, he said his prayers and went peacefully to bed.

"I'll get up early in the morning," he thought. "Then I can finish the shoes and perhaps sell them."

But when he arose, the pieces of cut leather were nowhere to be seen, and in their stead stood a pair of beautiful shoes all finished to the last seam and sewn so neatly that there was neither a flaw nor a false stitch in them. The shoemaker was

NOTES TO THE TELLER: The appearance of elves or other magical creatures to lend a helping hand is a frequent theme in folklore. Their kindness should always be repaid. Traditionally, this story is told during the Christmas season and speaks of the spirit of giving. It is a quiet story with a tone of mystery; it can be told as if it is a secret you are sharing.

amazed and did not know what to make of it, but he picked up the shoes and set them out for sale. Soon a man came and bought the shoes. And because he was so pleased with their fine workmanship, he paid more than the usual price for them. With this money, the shoemaker was able to buy enough leather for two pairs of shoes.

As before, he cut out the leather for the next day's sewing, laid it on his workbench, and went to bed. In the morning, there again were the shoes, two pairs this time! The hammer, the knife, the awl, the wax and twine, the needles and pegs, still lay about on the workbench as if someone had been working there, but no one could be seen. The shoemaker didn't know how such a thing could happen, but he was glad it happened all the same. Again he was lucky enough to sell the shoes for more than the usual price, and this time he was able to buy enough leather for four pairs of shoes.

Well, so it went on. Night after night he cut out the leather and laid it on his workbench. And morning after morning there stood a row of handsome shoes, ready to sell, ready to wear. And day after day, shoppers came and bought the shoes for such good prices that the shoemaker was able to buy more and more leather and sell more and more shoes. At last he was no longer poor. In fact, he became a well-to-do man with enough money in his pockets to buy whatever he needed. Then one evening—it was not long before Christmas—the shoemaker, after laying out the leather for many pairs of shoes, went to his wife and said, "What do you think if we stay up all night tonight, hiding? If we can, I want to watch and see who or what it is that is so good to us and comes every night to make the shoes."

"Yes," said his wife, "let us try to stay awake and see. I too would really like to find out who it is."

They lit a long candle and set it on a table, then hid behind the curtain that hung over the door. There they waited, struggling with sleep, until at last, just at midnight, came two stout little elves wearing ragged and tattered clothes that barely covered them. Barefoot themselves, the little creatures quickly sprang up on the workbench and began making shoes. They worked so swiftly and skillfully with little nimble fingers—piercing and punching and sewing, pegging and pounding—that the man and his wife could hardly believe their eyes.

And so the little elves worked on with tiny flying fingers and didn't stop for a moment until all the shoes were finished down to the last stitch and peg. Then, in a twinkling, they leapt up and ran away. Next morning the woman said, "Husband, what I was going to say, those little elves have made us rich—so to show our thanks would be no more than right. They run around, poor little things, all bare and must surely freeze. Do you know what? I will make them some clothes and knit them each a pair of stockings. You can make them each a pair of little shoes."

Oh, yes, the shoemaker would gladly do that. And so one evening, when everything was ready, they laid out their presents instead of the cutout leather, then hid once more behind the curtain and waited to see what the little creatures would do.

At midnight, there came the two little elves, skipping along, ready to sit down and work as usual. They looked, but saw no leather anywhere. They looked again and spied the row of little garments lying on the workbench: two little shirts and jerkins, two pairs of breeches, two peaked hats, four little stockings, and four tiny shoes with pointed toes. At first they seemed puzzled, as though wondering what these things were for, but then, when they understood that the clothes were meant for them, they were filled with joy. Quickly they picked up one little garment after another, dressing themselves with lightning speed; and all the time they laughed with delight and sang:

Now we are smart gentlemen,
Why should we ever work again?

When they were fully dressed, from peaked hats to pointy toes, they began to skip and run around like wild, so glad and gleeful were they. There seemed to be no end to their capers as they leapt over the chairs, and ran among the shelves and benches, but at last, after spinning round and round like tiny tops, they clasped hands and went dancing out the door.

They never came back, but the shoemaker and his wife were always lucky after that, and they never forgot the two little elves who had helped them in their time of need.

SOURCE: *Based on the version of the German folktale from* More Tales from Grimm, *translated by Wanda Gag (Coward-McCann, 1947).*

The Elves and the Shoemaker

STORY PLAN   GRADE LEVELS 1–3

Objectives

A) Provide students the opportunity to respond individually to literature through an open-ended discussion.

B) Assess students' listening comprehension, including their ability to visualize, through an arts-and-crafts activity.

C) Increase students' speaking ability by retelling the story and performing parts of the story.

D) Provide opportunities for reading similar stories by including several versions of "The Elves and the Shoemaker," other tales from Grimm, other multicultural tales of "little people" in the classroom library.

E) Encourage students to write by using their sense of "The Elves and the Shoemaker" to create a new episode for the elves featured in the story.

Activities

A) DISCUSSION: After telling the story the very first time, lead the students in an open-ended discussion that encourages divergent thinking. There are no right or wrong answers, no literal recall questions. Ask leading questions, such as:

- What was the most important part of the story to you? Why?
- What part of the story did you like the best? Why?
- What was the scariest (funniest, most beautiful) part? Why?

You might notice that in this particular story, there are some big ideas, such as the value of faith, hard work, and gratitude, for example. And the elves? What is their symbolic significance? Do they perhaps, represent the resilience of the human spirit, our innate vitality? Or just wishful thinking?

See if your students can address some of the bigger concepts in this sturdy folktale by asking them why people told this story to one another.

B) ARTS AND CRAFTS: Tell the story a second time and ask the students to pay particular attention to the description of the elves.

Then ask the students to draw lifelike pictures of the two elves as they were first seen in the story. One of the values of storytelling is that the students do not see any book illustrations and must visualize the characters for themselves. For the greatest amount of individual creativity, do not allow the students to discuss the details of the elves or to look at one another's illustrations until they are finished. Cut these out.

Ask some students (as an optional, small-group activity) to create new paper clothes for the elves. These can be of any description, as long as they are what the shoemaker and his wife might have made. Use tabs on the paper clothes and fit them to some of the cutout elves. Glue these elves to flat sticks to create a series of stick puppets with a change of wardrobe.

C) PLAYING THE STORY: Now the elves are ready to perform. Ask students to take turns performing the last scene of the story— when the elves come in and find their new clothes and dance around the shop and off into the night. Encourage students' own language as the "elves" talk to one another.

D) READING: Now it is time for the book versions of the story. Display illustrated versions of the elves, pointing out the different artists' interpretations of the elves, the other story characters, and the story settings. Arrange other books featuring elves and "little people" from many cultures as part of the story cycle. Ask students to read and tell these stories to one another.

E) WRITING: Ask students to write the next episode for "The Elves and the Shoemaker" but call it "The Elves and the _____?" Direct students in imagining what might happen next to the little elves. Think about the characteristics of the elves and their magical abilities. Small groups of students might work together on this assignment and later use the stick puppets to perform the next adventure in the ongoing saga of the two elves for the entire class.

The
Three
Bears
(Traditional)

NCE UPON A TIME THERE WERE three bears and they lived together in a house of their own deep in the forest. There was a wee, tiny, little bear. And there was a middle-size bear. And the other was a great, huge bear. And each had a pot for his porridge. There was a little, tiny pot for the little, tiny bear. There was a medium-size pot for the medium-size bear. And there was a great, huge pot for the great, huge bear. And each of them had his own chair to sit in: a little chair for the little, small, wee bear, and a middle-size chair for the middle-size bear, and a great, big chair for the great, big bear. And they all had their bed to sleep in: a little bed for the little, small, wee bear, a middle-size bed for the

---

NOTES TO THE TELLER: This is such a well-known story—easy to learn, easy to tell. Because you know it well, be sure to really see it again in your mind's eye. As you speak the different bears' dialogue, use a clearly distinct voice for each bear and be consistent with each repetition of that voice. You may have to rehearse the voices.

Children enjoy some pantomime with storytelling. This story lends itself easily to pantomime (eating the porridge, sitting in the chairs). These full-body gestures are also extra clues to meaning for the young child.

---

middle-size bear, and a great, big bed for the great, big bear.

One day, after they had made the porridge for their breakfasts, and poured it into their porridge pots, they walked out into the wood while their porridge was cooling, that they might not burn their mouths by beginning to eat it too soon. And while they were walking, a little girl named Goldilocks came to the house. She looked in at the window, and then she peeped in at the keyhole; seeing nobody in the house, she lifted the latch. The door was not fastened, because the bears were good bears, who did nobody any harm and never suspected that anybody would harm them. So Goldilocks opened the door and went in; and well-pleased she was when she saw the porridge on the table. If she had been a good little girl, she would have waited till the bears came home, and then, perhaps, they would have asked her to breakfast; for they were good bears—a little rough or so, as the manner of bears is, but for all that very good-natured and hospitable. But she set about helping herself.

So first she tasted the porridge of the great, huge bear, and that was too hot for her; and she said a bad word about that. And then she tasted the porridge of the middle bear, and that was too cold for her; and she said bad words about that too. And then she went to the porridge of the little, small, wee bear, and tasted that. She found it was neither too hot nor too cold but just right, and she liked it so well that she ate it all up; but the naughty girl said a bad word about the little porridge pot, because it did not hold enough for her.

Then Goldilocks sat down in the chair of the great, huge bear, and that was too hard for her. And then she sat down in the chair of the middle bear, and that was too soft for her. And then she sat down in the chair of the little, small, wee bear, and that was neither too hard nor too soft but just right. So she seated herself in it, and there she sat till the bottom of the chair came out, and down she came, *plump* to the ground. And the naughty girl said a wicked word about that too.

Then Goldilocks went upstairs into the bedchamber in which the three bears slept. At first she lay down upon the bed of the great, huge bear; but that was too high at the head for her. And next she lay down upon the bed of the middle bear; and that was too high at the foot for her. And then she lay down upon the bed of the little, small, wee bear; and that was neither too high at the head nor at the foot but just right. So she covered herself up comfortably and lay there till she fell fast asleep.

By this time the three bears thought their porridge would be cool enough, so they came home to breakfast. Now Goldilocks had left the spoon of the great, huge bear standing in his porridge.

"Somebody has been at my porridge!" said the great, huge bear in his great, rough, gruff voice. And when the middle bear looked at his, he saw the spoon was standing in his porridge too. They were wooden spoons; if they had been silver ones, the naughty little girl would have put them in her pocket.

"Somebody has been at my porridge!" said the middle bear in his middle voice.

Then the little, small, wee bear looked at his, and there was the spoon in the porridge pot, but the porridge was all gone.

"Somebody has been at my porridge and has eaten it all up!" said the little, small, wee bear in his little, small, wee voice.

Upon this the three bears, seeing that someone had entered their house and eaten up the little, small, wee bear's breakfast, began to look about them. Now Goldilocks had not put the hard cushion straight when she rose from the chair of the great, huge bear.

"Somebody has been sitting in my chair!" said the great, huge bear in his great, rough, gruff voice.

And Goldilocks had squashed down the soft cushion of the middle bear.

"Somebody has been sitting in my chair!" said the middle bear in his middle voice.

And you know what Goldilocks had done to the third chair. "Somebody has been sitting in my chair and has sat the bottom out of it!" said the little, small, wee bear in his little, small, wee voice.

Then the three bears thought it necessary to search further; so they went upstairs into their bedchamber. Now Goldilocks had pulled the pillow of the great, huge bear out of its place.

"Somebody has been lying in my bed!" said the great, huge bear in his great, rough, gruff voice.

And Goldilocks had pulled the bolster of the middle bear out of its place.

"Somebody has been lying in my bed!" said the middle bear in his middle voice.

And when the little, small, wee bear came to look at his bed, there was the bolster in its place and the pillow in its place upon the bolster. And upon the pillow was the little girl's head—which was not in its place, for she had no business there.

"Somebody has been lying in my bed—and here she is!" said the little, small, wee bear, in his little, small, wee voice.

Goldilocks had heard in her sleep the great, rough, gruff voice of the great, huge bear, but she was so fast asleep that it was no more to her than the roaring of wind or the rumbling of thunder. And then she heard the middle voice of the middle bear, but it was only as if she had heard someone speaking in a dream. But when she heard the little, small, wee voice of the little, small, wee bear, it was so sharp, and so shrill, that it awakened her at once. Up she started, and when she saw the three bears on one side of the bed, she tumbled out the other and ran to the window. Now the window was open, because the three bears, being good, tidy bears, always opened their bedchamber window when they got up in the morning. Out the little girl jumped; and whether she ran into the wood and was lost there or found her way out of the wood and was taken by the constable and sent to the House of Correction, I cannot tell. But the three bears never saw anything more of her.

SOURCE: Based on the version of the English folktale from English Fairy Tales, *collected and retold by Joseph Jacobs (Putnam, 1898).*

The Three Bears (Traditional)

STORY PLAN   GRADE LEVEL: K–3

Objectives

A) Allow the students to develop speaking ability by helping to tell the story.

B) Encourage students' self-expression by acting out the story.

C) Encourage students to further "play the story" by arts-and-crafts activity and additional performances.

D) Provide opportunities for reading by displaying many illustrated versions of "The Three Bears" in the classroom library.

E) Encourage independent thinking by asking the students to retell the story from the baby bear's point of view.

Activities

A) PARTICIPATION STORYTELLING: Tell the story once. With the second telling, ask the students to join in for the speaking parts.

B) PLAYING THE STORY: Tell the story a third time, telling the students that some students will be selected to play the story. The students will then know the story sequence well enough to act it out with very little prompting. Simply ask, "Who would like to be Goldilocks?" "Who would like to be the Middle Bear?" and so on. Be sure to lay out the stage settings somewhere in the classroom (where the beds are, the chairs, the bowls). These could be imaginary or real props.

C) ARTS AND CRAFTS: Ask the students to bring teddy bears from home or make bear puppets. Draw or paint large pictures of the three bears' house. Choose several of the backdrop drawings (paintings) to put on a puppet/teddy bear play of the story. A doll or puppet or another stuffed animal could be Goldilocks. Make sure that many children get a turn to play and have the opportunity to continue playing this story in the playhouse or play area.

D) READING: Now that the students have had free rein visualizing the story, display many picture-book versions of the tale. Ask students to read from the books and read aloud from these book versions yourself.

E) INDEPENDENT THINKING: Ask students to retell the story from the small bear's point of view. You might have to start them out with a monologue: "I woke up and went downstairs. 'Good morning,' I cheerfully said to Big Bear and Middle Bear, 'I'm famished!' 'In that case, I have some bad news,' said Middle Bear, 'the porridge I made is way too hot to eat right now. . . .' " Students could use the teddy bears or puppets to tell this monologue.

The Three Bears Jingle

Once upon a time
In a nursery rhyme
There were (1, 2, 3)
Three bears.

They all went a-walkin'
In the deep woods a-talkin'
When along came a girl
With (1, 2, 3) long, golden hair.

NOTES TO THE TELLER: This is a syncopated version of "The Three Bears" based on the beat in "Hey-Bob-a-Re-Ba." Sometimes called "The Jazzy Three Bears," this rendition changes beats and can be challenging. If in doubt, ask the students to help you. There is no right or wrong way to say this jingle, as long as you are consistent and enjoying yourself.

    The version here is abbreviated. Try adding the missing lines yourself. Use percussion instruments or simple hand-clapping to keep you on the beat.

She knocked on the door.
Ba-boom, ba-boom,
Boom, boom, boom.
But no one was there.

She went right in and
She had herself a ball,
Eatin' and sleepin' and
Rockin' and all.

She didn't care.
No one was there.
She ate all the porridge.
And she sat in the chair.

She went to sleep.
You know where.
....
....

Home came the three bears
Tired from the woods,
Ready to sit down
To some home-cooked goods.

"Someone's been eating
My porridge,"
Said the Papa Bear,
Said the Papa Bear.

"Someone's been eating
My porridge,"
Said the Mama Bear,
Said the Mama Bear.
"Hey, Mama, see there,
Someone has eaten
My porridge. Wah."

....

....

They went upstairs to
See what they could find.
And there was Goldilocks,
Asleep all the time.

Goldilocks woke up
And she broke up the party
And she boogied right
Out of there.

"Bye, bye, bye, bye, bye,"
Said the Papa Bear.

"Bye, bye, bye, bye, bye,"
Said the Mama Bear.

"Hey, Mama, see there,"
Said the wee, little bear,
"What kind of bear was
That there, huh?"

And so goes the story,
And so goes the story
Of the three little bears,
Yeah!

Source: White Horses and Whippoorwills, *Barbara Freeman and Connie Regan (The Folktellers, MTA Productions, Nashville, Tennessee, 1981). "Jazzy Three Bears" (traditional jingle) attributed to five-year-old Shoshanna Korsakov of Chattanooga, who says she learned it at day care.*

The Three Bears Jingle
STORY PLAN   GRADE LEVEL: 4–6

Objectives

A) Provide older students with an opportunity to use popular culture as a medium to reinterpret a traditional tale.

B) Provide older students with a young audience and at the same time create role models for the younger students to assist them in enjoying stories and the arts.

Activities

A) INDEPENDENT THINKING/PERFORMING ARTS: Ask students to make up a new version of "The Three Bears Jingle," using another musical beat. Students may work in small groups to produce this new version. It could be a rap or be based on another song with a distinctive and well-known beat. Instruments or background music, as well as body movements, could be part of the production.

B) PERFORMING ARTS: Ask the groups to perform their version of "The Three Bears Jingle" for the primary-grade classes. They will need to rehearse and provide simple costuming.

Three
Jovial
Huntsmen

There were three jovial huntsmen,
As I have heard men say,
And they would go a-hunting
Upon St. David's day.

And all the day they hunted,
Nothing did they find,
But a ship, a ship
A-sailing, sailing with the wind.

The first said it was a ship,
The second he said Nay,
The third said it was a house
With its chimney blown away.

NOTES TO THE TELLER: In a quiet room, this rhyme can be spellbinding. It's a good way to still a noisy group.

STORYTELLING: A GUIDE FOR TEACHERS

And all the night they hunted,
Nothing did they find,
But the moon a-gliding,
A-gliding with the wind.

The first said it was the moon,
The second he said Nay,
The third said it was a cheese
With half of it cut away.

And all the day they hunted,
Nothing did they find,
But a hedgehog in a bramble bush,
And that they left behind.

The first said it was a hedgehog,
The second he said Nay,
And the third said it was a pincushion
With the pins stuck in the wrong way.

And all the night they hunted,
Nothing did they find,
But a hare in a turnip field,
And that they left behind.

There were three jovial huntsmen,
As I have heard men say,
And they would go a-hunting
Upon St. David's day.

SOURCE: *Mother Goose rhymes.*

Three Jovial Huntsmen
STORY PLAN   K–2

Objectives

A) Provide students with the opportunity to enjoy the sound and music of language with choral reading.
B) Provide students with an opportunity to hear many Mother Goose and other multicultural nursery rhymes and so increase their cultural literacy.

Activities

A) CHORAL READING: Tell the rhyme a number of times. Ask the students to join in in quiet voices. Use your hands to give cues for phrasing, pausing, and volume.

B) READING: Expose the students to many editions of Mother Goose rhymes and multicultural nursery rhymes. To make the telling of the rhymes more like a game, play Mother Goose Marathon (MGM). Place the Mother Goose book(s) and other nursery-rhyme books on a table or on the floor in front of your class. Choose a child to come and pick up a book, any book. Ask the child to close his or her eyes and open the book to a random page. Ask the child to open his eyes and point to a rhyme on the pages that are open. You then say the rhyme; he says it with you; then the whole class says it together. Place the closed book on the floor again and ask another child to make a random selection. Youngsters love this simple game and are greatly motivated to pick up these books on their own and search for new rhymes.

Ma Lien
And
The
Magic
Brush

ONCE UPON A TIME IN ANCIENT
China there lived a poor peasant boy whose name was Ma Lien.
He worked hard in the fields every day and earned what he
could for the food he needed and a small hut for his shelter.
His greatest dream was to be an artist. But he had no money to
buy a brush.

Even without a brush, Ma Lien found a way to draw
pictures. He would scratch pictures of animals on the flat rocks
in the field using a sharp stone, or he would use his fingers to
draw in the wet sand along the river. When he was alone in his
small hut at night, he would draw pictures on his wall with a
piece of charcoal from his stove. Soon he had covered his walls
with all the things he had seen or could imagine.

Ma Lien's skill grew. When he would draw pictures of a
wolf or a chicken, the other animals thought that they were

---

*NOTES TO THE TELLER: For this story, it is important to visualize. See each scene in as
much detail as possible. You too have the power to make things become real—with
your voice!*

---

real. The sheep in the field would stay away from the wolf; a hawk would begin to circle around the chicken. But for all his scratchings, Ma Lien still did not have a brush.

One night, when Ma Lien was lying on his bed, looking at all the pictures around him on the walls of his room, he thought, *If only I had a brush, what wonderful pictures I could paint.*

The instant that Ma Lien had that thought, there was a flash of white light, and standing before the boy was an old wizard, with a long white beard that hung down all the way to the floor, leaning on a tall, twisted staff.

"Ma Lien," he said with a creaky voice, "you have great skill as a painter and you have worked very hard. Now you have earned a brush. Use it wisely, for it has great power." Saying this, he handed the trembling boy a bright, golden paintbrush with white bristles. Before Ma Lien could say a word, the wizard vanished.

Without wasting a second, Ma Lien went to a bare spot on his wall. He touched the brush to the wall and soon discovered that whatever color he thought, the brush would paint. He quickly painted a rooster with many colorful feathers. When he put the finishing touch on the last tail feather, the bird sprang from the wall to the windowsill, called out, "Cock-a-doodle-doo," and flew off into the night.

"Now I know why the wizard said this brush had great power," said Ma Lien. "Do not worry, old man. I will use it wisely."

The next morning when Ma Lien was walking to the mountain to gather firewood, he passed a rice paddy. There he saw a man and a young boy pulling a heavy plow to till the paddy. Ma Lien quickly went over to the wall of an old shed and painted a strong and healthy water buffalo. Again, when he finished, the beast leapt from the wall and with a low moo lumbered down to the paddy. Now, with the help of the buffalo, the man and his son soon had the paddy ready for planting.

Just at that moment the mandarin, the ruler of that land, came by, and seeing the power of Ma Lien's magic brush, ordered his men to seize the poor boy. When they had taken Ma Lien to the mandarin, he commanded the boy to paint a pile of silver coins for him. Ma Lien, remembering the wizard's words, refused, and the mandarin had him thrown in the dungeon with his other prisoners.

Ma Lien soon discovered that the other men had done no wrong, but had been imprisoned by the mandarin so that he could steal their lands. "Never fear," said the boy, "I will have us all free before too long." As the night passed, Ma Lien waited until the guard had dozed off. Then quickly he painted a door on the wall. The prisoners pushed against it, the door swung open and they fled into the night. The mandarin's men came chasing after Ma Lien, but the boy easily escaped on the fine horse he had painted for himself.

Ma Lien knew he would not be safe if he remained on the mandarin's lands, so he rode for many miles until he came to a strange village. Here he continued to help anyone he could with his magic brush. He painted buffaloes to help the farmers in their fields. He painted chickens for the farmers' wives, and he painted toys to keep the children happy. One day he came upon some farmers hard at work carrying buckets of water to their dried-up fields. "That work is much too hard for you," said Ma Lien, and he set about painting a fine waterwheel so that it would be easier to bring the water from the river into the fields. And so it was that Ma Lien and his wonderful brush became known throughout the land.

It wasn't long before the mandarin learned where Ma Lien was living. He sent his soldiers to the village, and when they found the boy, they seized him and dragged him back to the palace.

The mandarin instantly took away the brush and commanded that the boy be thrown into the dungeon. "Without the brush I don't think he will escape so easily," he laughed. Then he sent for the court painter and ordered him to paint a picture with the brush.

"What would you have me paint?"

"A tree," said the mandarin. "A tree with gold coins for leaves that will fall like the rain when I shake the branches."

The artist went right to work and soon had a fine tree with gold coins for leaves painted on the wall of the palace. But when the mandarin rushed to shake the tree he got no more than a bump on the head for his trouble. The tree was nothing but a painting on the wall.

Now the mandarin realized that only Ma Lien had the power to paint pictures that would become real. Sending for the boy, he spoke kindly to him. "Ma Lien," he said softly, "if you will paint but one picture for me I will give you your freedom." The boy, thinking of a way to trick the greedy man, agreed to do as he was asked.

The mandarin's eyes lit up with delight. He handed the brush to Ma Lien and said, "Paint me a mountain of pure gold." The boy went to work at once, painting a broad expanse of blue sea. The wide sea spread all across the wall.

"Why do you paint the sea?" demanded the mandarin. "I ordered a mountain of gold."

"I have not finished," said the boy quietly, and with that he painted a great gold mountain rising up out of the sea.

"Beautiful, beautiful!" cried the mandarin.

"Now paint me a ship so that I can sail to my mountain and bring back the gold."

In a twinkling, Ma Lien had painted a fine ship, worthy of a mandarin who was about to travel to a mountain of gold. The man wasted no time in hurrying aboard with a troop of his finest soldiers. The sail was raised and slowly the ship rode out to sea.

"Too slow, too slow!" shouted the mandarin. "Give us a

wind to speed us along." Obediently, Ma Lien painted a wind cloud. The wind came whistling down and the sails filled out. The wind ruffled the water and great waves rose about the ship.

"Too much, too much!" cried the mandarin angrily. "You will sink my ship." But Ma Lien payed no attention. He went right on painting storm clouds. Now the wind howled and shrieked, and the waves crashed about the ship. Then with a great *c-r-r-r-ack*, the ship split in two and sank in the stormy waters.

Once more Ma Lien returned to simple life with the peasants, always ready to help them with their work. And never again was he forced to use his magic brush for greed.

SOURCE: Based on the version by Hisako Kimishima, translated by Alvin Tresselt (Parents' Magazine Press, New York, 1968); originally published as Ma Lien Maho No Fude *(Kaisei Sha, Tokyo, Japan).*

Ma Lien and the Magic Brush
STORY PLAN   GRADE LEVEL 4–6

Objectives

A) Provide students with the opportunity to respond individually to literature with an open-ended discussion.

B) Assess students' ability to visualize and create new images through an art activity.

C) Increase students' ability to adapt the concepts in traditional literature to modern times with a writing assignment.

Activities

A) DISCUSSION: After telling the story the first time, lead the students in a discussion that encourages divergent thinking. Ask questions such as "What was the most important part of the story to you? Why?" "What was the best part of the story? Why?" This story discusses certain ethical and social values. You might ask the students why this story was told in China.

B) ARTS: Give each student a brush, watercolors, water, and matte paper. After a brief discussion of watercolor techniques, remind the students to use the brush "wisely." Ask them to think of what they would paint if their brush had the power to make their painting real and why they would select such a thing(s). Ask them to write the reasons for their painting on a separate sheet of paper or tell these reasons to a partner. Display and discuss the paintings with the entire class.

C) WRITING: Ask the students to adapt this traditional story to your present school community. If Ma Lien were alive today in your community, who would try to capture him and what would they make him paint? How would Ma Lien escape? How would he live the rest of his life?

Anansi The Spider, Or How The Spider Got A Small Waist

LONG AGO IN A CONTINENT called Africa, there lived first spider, and first spider's name was Kwaku Anansi. Now what Anansi liked to do best of all was to eat. He liked to eat just about everything. And one day, he heard there was to be a feast in Diabee. And then Anansi heard that there was to be a feast the same day in Kibbes.

Now at a feast you can eat as much as you want, and Anansi didn't know which feast to go to. So he thought and thought and thought. And then he had an idea. He called his sons and he had them put a string around his middle and one went up to Diabee and one went to Kibbes. And he told them to pull on the string when the food was served.

Then Anansi waited and waited, and at last he felt a pull

Notes to the Teller: This West African story is an example of a "pourquoi" tale, one that explains how things came to be the way they are today. Kwaku Anansi, the spider, is a delightful trickster character from the Ashanti people; he is often shrewd but just as often is outsmarted by his own greed. Stories have many layers of meaning. This particular one teaches values with a wonderful good humor. Tell it quickly—with gusto. It should be over before the students really know what happened.

on the string—up towards Diabee—and he started out. But he hadn't gone very far when he felt a pull in the other direction—towards Kibbes. And both boys were pulling so hard on the string that Anansi was stuck right there in the middle.

Well, the boys waited until the food had been served and put away, and then they came down to see what had happened to their father. But he didn't look the same. Where that string had gone around his center, his body was now divided into two parts.

And that is the way all spiders have remained. If you don't believe me, go look at a spider and you'll see for yourself; that's how all spiders are to this very day.

SOURCE: Based on the version of the African folktale from The Hat-Shaking Dance, *collected by Harold Courlander (Harcourt, 1957).*

How the Spider Got a Small Waist

STORY PLAN   GRADE LEVEL: 2–4

Objectives

A) Provide students with an opportunity to learn a cycle of similar tales and increase their cultural literacy.

B) Research the current scientific findings about spiders as a species.

C) Allow the students to use both scientific information and their imaginations to write their own spider story.

Activities

A) READING: Collect and display a cycle of African and Caribbean Anansi stories in the classroom. So many of these stories exist that they are plentiful in the folktale selections in any children's library. Too often they go untold. Assign small groups of students to read the same story and tell it to the class.

B) RESEARCH: Collect nonfiction books about spiders. Small groups can make reports on different types of spiders. You might even have a pet spider in the room—he or she could be Anansi.

C) WRITING: Ask the students to write an original or true story about a spider. Ask the children to illustrate their story using the illustrations and photographs from the folktale books and the nonfiction books.

Josefina

THERE WAS A MAID NAMED Josefina. She worked in a very rich house. This family was so rich that the milk they bought in the morning was not used up by nighttime. So whatever was left over they gave to Josefina. Josefina made very good use of this. She would take the milk to market every day and sell it.

One day they gave her more milk than ever. Josefina was dancing with joy on the way to the market. She would think of something and she would skip and jump. Her mind was far away. She did not remember that she was carrying the milk. This is what she was saying to herself:

"When I sell this *leche* (that's milk) I'll buy a nice big *gallina* (that's a hen), and that hen will give me *muchos muchos*

NOTES TO THE TELLER: Counting your chickens before they hatch, dreaming of your trade on the way to market, doesn't always pay off. This familiar bit of folk wisdom is given here in a particularly Mexican version with Spanish words introduced throughout the story. Stories are one way to introduce the customs and languages of a variety of cultures. Be sure to learn the correct pronunciation of these words before you tell this story.

huevos (many eggs), and I'll sell them quickly. And with the money I get, I'll buy, you know what? *Uno puerco* (that's a pig). And I'll feed him acorn and barley, and when he gets big and fat, I'll sell him. And with the money I get, I'll buy *una vaca* (that's a cow). No, *dos vacas!* And what will those *vacas* give me? Milk, lots of milk. And what will I do with that milk? I'll take it to market and sell it. I will be selling the milk from my very own cows."

That thought excited her so much that she jumped higher than ever and, oh, she tripped. And she fell. And all her dreams came to nothing. There she sat, in the middle of the street, and she was saying:

"*Adios gallinas, adios huevos, adios puerco, adios vacas, adios leche.*" And to you I say, "*Adios amigos.*"

SOURCE: *Based on the version of the Mexican folktale from* The Boy Who Could Do Anything, *collected and retold by Anita Brenner (Addison-Wesley, 1942).*

Josefina
STORY PLAN   GRADE LEVEL: 3–6

Objectives

A) Provide bilingual exposure for all the students by telling this story in Spanish.

B) Increase cultural appreciation and tell other versions of the story from around the world.

C) Expose students to multilingual tellings of this story and story variants.

Activities

A) RETELLING THE STORY: Tell the story in Spanish or play a recording of the story told in Spanish by a community member.

B) READING: Collect multicultural story types for the classroom library. Ask students to read or tell these stories to the class.

C) ART: Make a felt board and ask students to draw and cut the many objects from this story and others like it. Create a storyboard for telling and retelling the story in many languages. The felt objects are context clues to meaning for bilingual adults and students. This particular story, because it deals with so many common objects and animals, adapts very well to learning multilingual vocabularies.

Daphne
And
Apollo

YOU REMEMBER THAT CUPID, THE god of love and mischief, had two kinds of arrows, one made of lead and one made of gold. Do you recall what would happen if Cupid struck someone in the heart with a lead arrow? That's right, the person he struck would hate the next individual he or she saw. And what would happen if Cupid struck someone in the heart with an arrow from his quiver that was made of gold? That's right, the person struck with a golden arrow would have no choice but to fall in love with the very next person that he or she saw.

Now, one day Cupid was bored, flying around in the sky with his quiver full of arrows. He was ready for some mischief. Who should he hit with one of his arrows? Just then, Cupid spied the great god Apollo himself in his chariot, pulling the

---

NOTES TO THE TELLER: This story is told in my own language. You will see the voice that I sometimes bring to a story—especially if I want to appeal to a particular group of students. This is the prerogative of any storyteller—to tell it your way! For comparison and contrast, read Bulfinch's Mythology *for another version of the same tale.*

---

golden sun in its daily journey across the heavens. Cupid could not resist such a target. He pulled back his small bow, fitted it with a golden arrow, and took aim. He struck Apollo directly in the heart.

Apollo didn't quite know what had happened, but he suddenly felt more radiant than even the sun god usually feels. He glowed all over. Looking down from the heavens on the earth below, he saw a figure moving in the forest. It chanced to be Daphne, a beautiful but shy wood nymph.

Daphne loved to frequent the darkest and quietest parts of her thick, green forest. She had pledged herself to Diana the huntress and enjoyed the freedom of the woods. She wore simple garments, and her unkempt hair was often decorated with flowers. Apollo saw her as she darted into a clearing to pick some wildflowers. Because of Cupid's golden arrow, he could not resist her. He jumped from his chariot and landed easily in the clearing below.

Daphne was terrified by the great god suddenly appearing next to her. He was so bright, radiant with curly black hair and dark glowing eyes. She turned immediately and began to run, to hide. She did not trust the gods.

Apollo called out to her. He begged her to understand that he meant her no harm. He wanted to be her friend, to woo her. He ran after her to explain; he could not bear to see her running away. But Daphne did not stop; she fled in terror.

She knew the secret pathways of the forest and the hidden trails. But Apollo was the sun god and had great strength and speed. He easily followed her and uprooted the underbrush and saplings to gain sight of her. This frightened Daphne even more. Now she feared for her very life. She heard Apollo shouting to her but did not hear his words. His voice shattered her quiet world. His strength was destroying it. She ran like a cornered animal. She did not know that he was saying that he loved her.

When it seemed that Apollo would catch up to her, she called out to her father, Peneus, the god of a nearby waterway. "Peneus, help me! I am in danger!" Her father heard her cry—and just in time.

Apollo now reached out for her and touched the bark of a tree. He searched for her hand and grasped a handful of twigs. He touched her hair and felt fresh, green leaves. For Daphne had become a newly formed tree, rooted to the ground. Apollo stayed by the tree for a long time, gazing at its beauty. He called this the laurel tree.

Apollo never forgot his love for Daphne. Every hero returning from battle and every winner in the Olympic games Apollo crowned with his highest honor, a branch from the laurel tree.

SOURCE: Retold by Catharine Farrell, based on her recollection of her first storytelling experience, San Francisco, 1967.

Daphne and Apollo

STORY PLAN   GRADE LEVELS: 6–9

If I had known in 1967 what I know now, I would have planned the following lesson for my students in ninth-grade English.

Objectives

A) Develop the students' ability to visualize details of the characters in a story.

B) Increase students' ability to identify with characters in a story.

C) Research existing remnants of the myth in international culture and so enhance students' cultural literacy.

D) Provide the opportunity to read and tell a similar myth from other cultures.

Activities

A) ART: Ask students to draw Daphne and Apollo in detail according to their own imagination. Display these drawings in class. Bind in a class book.

B) WRITING: Ask students to write Daphne's thoughts as a newly formed tree. Create this monologue in draft form. Read aloud and continue to write in small groups. Groups will select scripts to present to the whole class as a tree monologue; spoken presentations will be in character. All interpretations are acceptable—from tragic to humorous to idyllic.

C) RESEARCH: Ask students to conduct library research on the following:

    1. A female runner who has won an Olympic gold medal. Prepare a brief biography and report for the class.

    2. Artwork depicting Apollo or Daphne or both (for example, Bernini's famous statue). Bring examples of the artwork to display in class. Compare and contrast the collected artwork with the students' own artistic interpretations.

CATHARINE FARRELL, MLS, is the president and founder of Word Weaving, Inc., a nonprofit educational corporation. She has been a language-arts classroom teacher, librarian, storyteller, and university lecturer in the San Francisco Bay Area for more than twenty-five years. She has served as a consultant to the California State Department of Education in Sacramento, been awarded grants from the Zellerbach Family Fund, San Francisco, and developed language-arts curricula for preschool through high school.

Ms. Farrell designed the Word Weaving Storytelling Project to encourage teachers at all levels to learn and enjoy the art. She based its training program, and its materials, on her experience with storytelling and her belief in it.

For information about the Word Weaving Storytelling Training Program and materials, please write to Word Weaving, Inc., 372 Florin Rd., Suite 122, Sacramento, CA 95831.